A Sense Of Reason

poetry pt today

A Sense Of Reason

Edited by Suzy Walton

First published in Great Britain in 2001 by Poetry
Today, an imprint of
Penhaligon Page Ltd, Remus House, Coltsfoot Drive,
Woodston, Peterborough. PE2 9JX

© Copyright Contributors 2001

All rights reserved. No part of this publication may be
reproduced, stored in a retrieval system, or transmitted
in any form or by any means, without prior permission
from the author(s).

A Catalogue record for this book is available from the
British Library

ISBN 1 86226 673 5

Typesetting and layout, Penhaligon Page Ltd, England.
Printed and bound by Forward Press Ltd, England

Foreword

A Sense Of Reason is a compilation of poetry, featuring some of our finest poets. This book gives an insight into the essence of modern living and deals with the reality of life today. We think we have created an anthology with a universal appeal.

There are many technical aspects to the writing of poetry and *A Sense Of Reason* contains free verse and examples of more structured work from a wealth of talented poets.

Poetry is a coat of many colours. Today's poets write in a limitless array of styles: traditional rhyming poetry is as alive and kicking today as modern free verse. Language ranges from easily accessible to intricate and elusive.

Poems have a lot to offer in our fast-paced 'instant' world. Reading poems gives us an opportunity to sit back and explore ourselves and the world around us.

Contents

Title	Author	Page
Mothers	Ron Cousins	1
Ode To Ann	Frank Littlewood	2
A Rhyme In Time	Margaret Batchelor	3
Stars	Ruth Shallard	4
My Eternal Love	Robert Beach	5
Luminous Interludes	Flossie	6
Gym	Sara Patterson	7
Odd Ditties Or Oddities	Jackie Stubington	8
Beyond: Reaching	Ronald D Lush	9
The Essence Of Poetry	Veronica Quainton	10
An Appointment With The Doctor	Les Orme	11
The Special Things In Life!	Lynne Doyle	12
An Image Of Love	Neata Todd	13
Modern Mouse	Val Stephenson	14
Rejected Love	Linda Wright	15
All Terrain Vehicle . . . From Hell!	Lyndsey Power	16
Out Of Reach	Lorna Marlow	18
Smokescreen	Roger James Brawn	19
Sweet Love	K Morrison	20
Dad's Love In The Rainbow	Alison McColgan	21
Smiles	Angela Pritchard	22
You	Emmalene Maguire	23
The Swan	Katie Smith	24
Time For Children	Joyce Dawn Willis	25
God's Anguish	John A Mills	26
When I Was Joseph . . .	Rachael Mary Widdrington	27
Adoration	Christine Hare	28
Stand In Lover	Roy Barker	29
Ode To Be Loved Again	Myra Granville	30
John-Paul	Bess Langley	31
So Many Ways	Patricia Whittle	32
Flexible Love	Hazel Mills	33
Together	Judith Rawlings	34
Faith Can!	Elaine Smicle-Thompson	35
Shadows In The Trees	Patti Ryall	36

Rhyme Time	Betty Nevell	37
Dreaming	Pamela Evans	38
A Rhyme In Time	Kath Aust	39
A Rhyme On Time!	Carole Hackett	40
A Strange Recital	Ralph C Davis	41
A Mixed Bag	Joyce Buksh	42
Mugs Are For Coffee	Gillian M Morphy	43
Time	Margaret Whitton	44
Sport	Margaret McDonald	45
Their Gift	Sue Cockayne	46
Let's Dance	Pam Redmond	48
Blackbird	Joan Tompkins	49
The Loner	Nan Downs	50
Clouds	Mary Lawson	51
In Favour Of Rhyme	Olive Miller	52
Impressions:		
Monday Morning; 9.35	Sandra MacLean	53
Wilfred	Geraldine Laker	54
The Boy Whose Eyes Fell Out	Mark Follows	55
Acceptance (Being Me)	Anne Gray	56
Stop A While	Jean D Smith	57
If Only I Knew	Ken Watts	58
Ode To Those Who Were Lost	Gemma King	59
Dorothy Ann	Albert Cole	60
Good Times	Jo Williams	61
Why Is My Bag So Heavy?	Rod Remnant	62
I Met Him One Morning	Les Parnell	64
Nemesis	Vera Watson	66
Horn Of Plenty	Robert D Hayward	67
Cats	Suzanne L Shepherd	68
The Hard Part Of Art	Roger Mather	69
The Ant-Agonist	José Evelyn Wilcox	70
Taxi Driver	P J Rowlands	71
Was And Is	May Walker	72
My Love	Linda Sibley	73
Angel Eyes	Abida Haidar	74
Bring Back Pictures In The Fire	Allan Bula	75
Eve Of Construction	Judy Studd	76

Title	Author	Page
Rhyme In Time	Den Evans	78
Progress	Mary Neill	79
The Scone Song	Waddington Minge	80
A Rhyme In Time	Joyce Metcalfe	81
Times Gone By	Robert Gerald	82
Don't Know It, Poet	June Davies	83
Ode To Mr Forrest ~ A Lousy Driver	Vivienne Rae Nolan	84
At The Airport	Phil Harvey	85
I Wish	Jenny Brownjohn	86
Rhyme	John Clancy	87
In Such A Place	Peter English	88
A Hebridean Holiday	Sara Newby	89
Autumn Clean-Up	Irene Pierce	90
Time	Gwen Mason	91
A Rocket For Guy	Samantha Warburton	92
For Her	Mike Monaghan	93
A Faraway Land	Jackie Annetts	94
Tangled Love	Amanda Clapp	95
Berwick Church, Sussex	R Cunningham	96
Grandad	Karen Lawson	97
Tiger	M Campbell	98
The Oboe Player	Ralph C Davis	99
A Lily's Gilt	Angus Richmond	100
The Weekend Break	Eileen Burton	101
The Now	Yenti	102
Friends	Marisa Greenaway	103
Reflections On The Millennium	Joan Leahy	104
Live For The Day	Elizabeth Myra Crellin	105
The Tooth Fairy	Graham John	106
A Birthday Thought	Pauline Cunningham	107
Within Verona's Walls	George Puttock	108
City Of Fear	Mary P Linney	109

Mothers

You can't put a price on a *mother's* worth
Takes care and looks after you as well as give birth
She feeds and clothes you, changes your nappy
Gives you hugs and kisses to keep you happy
Washes and changes you before putting to bed
Soothes and nurses when you have a bad head
Listens at night to make sure you're breathing
Rubs stuff on your gums when you start teething
Pushes the pram and sings you a song
Teaches you the value of right and what's wrong
Takes you to school when you start your first day
Washes the dirt out of the your clothes when you've been out to play
She's there whenever you have a disaster
Covers your wound with a bandage or sticking plaster
Watches you grow up, even worries when you're older
Always there if you ever need her shoulder
Forever willing, always trying her best
Still thinks of you when you've flown the nest
Now I have children it would be nice to discover
That I've taken good care of them just like you *Mother*

Ron Cousins

Ode To Ann

Concealed within the very core of me,
Among my most profound and secret things,
Which rarely surface save in wanderings
Through dreams and then so often flee
Into oblivion, lurks a tiny word,
A pronoun on the unromantic tongue
Of old grammarians, hidden until stung
To daylight by my yearning vision, stirred
By Her, long sought and now in sequel found,
The lady of those dreams, whose Her awakes
The longed for Her in me, the Her that takes
No plural 's' and always must be crowned
With that defining capital: the Her
To whom beyond all others I defer

Frank Littlewood

A Rhyme In Time

A time for everything under the sun
    A time to dream and a time for fun
A time to laugh and a time to cry
    A time to relax and a time to fly
A time to get busy and a time to earn
    Then spend and spend until you learn
That the best things in life are not bought with money
No need to toil, no need to worry
If you have friends and love, so much to give
And give and give again
Of yourself and your love.
That's when you will gain
    Happiness

    Margaret Batchelor

Stars

They hang like lamps above the land,
Unchanging, plac'd by God's own Hand.

Since dawn of time seas have been sailed,
With stars their guide that never failed.

From Hand Divine they have their source:
That Hand alone can stay their course.

Ruth Shallard

My Eternal Love

My love for you will always be
Higher than the mountains
And deeper than the sea
Whene'er I need someone to care
You are the one who's always there
Since first we met I have depended on you
You are my friend loyal and true
Time and space cannot keep us apart
I will love you always with all my heart
We are two soulmates who share one life
Brought together as husband and wife
You are my future, you are my past
You are my beginning, you are my last
And that's the way it will always be
As we drift along to eternity
On and on until the end of time
I am yours and you are mine
You are to me a gift from above
And you will always be
My eternal love.

Robert Beach

Luminous Interludes

Just look around you,
Perhaps you will see
Unwritten poems
That some day may be.

You can walk by the ocean
Leaving imprints in sand,
But the blessings you leave
Will be written by hand.

Exploring outer limits of rhyme
Or marriage of free verse and prose,
Put your pen to the paper,
Imagery, metaphor compose.

You may be inspired at dawn,
Thoughts enter into your head,
Or moonlight madness
Invades your spirit instead.

You may hear luminous words
Spoken by eloquent preachers,
Or words of knowledge and wisdom
Taught by educated teachers.

There are poems plucked from mid air,
Vivid or subtle scenes,
Thoughts of purity or passion,
Write down just what you mean.

Poetry invokes free expression
Of love, peace, joy, hurts, or fears,
Fertile opportunities and horizons
Throughout literary years.

Flossie

Gym

I go to the gym every day
I'm told it's good for me
I'm told it makes you feel better
But this I've yet to see

I step onto the treadmill
It will not slow its pace
I wanted to have a walk
But it decided to race

So I go onto the stepper
And climb and climb for hours
With all the floors it says I've done
I must have climbed ten towers!

I decide to go and do some rowing
But I never do get wet
Although when it gets harder
I break into a sweat

I go onto the strength machines
I can lift a lot of weight
I don't mind doing bicep pulls
But tricep dips I hate

I go to the gym every day
Muscles I'm trying to build
And after an hour or two workout
With satisfaction I am filled

Although my body's aching
I'm sweaty and quite hot
They tell me it will be worth it
When a fit body I have got!

Sarah Patterson

Odd Ditties Or Oddities

I think it would be very stunning
To observe a running bean that's running.
Or maybe to see a sweet, sweetpea,
Taking sugar in its tea.

A dandelion dressing up?
A baby drinking from a buttercup?
A rose arising to the summer sky.
Tell me, for how long does a weeping willow cry?

Do you think bluebells get down in the dumps?
Perhaps even camels can have the hump.
I wonder how these things can be.
It really is quite strange to me.

    Jackie Stubington

Beyond: Reaching

Stretched upon the expanse of space
Curtain cords and silken lace.
Filtered light from sun and moon
This time moves by far too soon.
A veil of memory shutters out
Some distant life without a doubt.
Forgotten moments from days gone by
I wonder why, I wonder why.
Is there hope in these short hours
To grow and grow like springtime flowers,
And return to dust from whence we came.
Then renew our lives and be the same.
To drift and be a nothingness,
Or wander through some new wilderness.
I wonder if, I wonder if
Beyond is there a greater gift?

Ronald D Lush

The Essence Of Poetry

My honest opinion I think you want to know
A poem that doesn't rhyme is hard to follow
You don't know where to stop or worse where to start
It's difficult to see what line belongs to which part
It's pleasant to recite when it flows off the tongue
When each line fits together one by one
The words that paint a picture that touches the soul
That brings it all together as part of the whole
As you read the words you want to feel peace
Not wondering when it will all cease
Each line an inspiration from God above
Filled with His beauty, goodness and love
Surely this is real poetry for all to enjoy
Rather than having read it, concluding oh why!

Veronica Quainton

An Appointment With The Doctor

I needed to see the doctor 'cause I was feeling very ill
It wasn't for his sympathy but a make me better pill
I spoke to the receptionist and told her of my pain
She said, 'Unless you're dying sir, you'll have to call again.'
I phoned again and oh! What joy, an appointment could be mine
The receptionist said, 'We have a space, you can come in two
						weeks' time.'
When at last the appointment came I duly staggered in
The doctor said, 'You're looking well,' but he hid a wily grin
I told him I was in great pain, it was just below the rib
He said, 'It all feels fine to me,' but it sounded rather glib
So there it was I'd been dismissed I had to leave you see
Without some make me better pills and a lack of sympathy.

Les Orme

The Special Things In Life!

The special things in life ~
Are the things we get for free!
Moments we take for granted,
That mean the world to me!

Like a loving hug at bedtime,
Or a funny joke that was told,
These are special things to treasure,
More than pots of silver and gold!

To have a family to be loved by
And to care for when they need you.
And to make friends with your neighbours
And to share a laugh or two.

It's worth more than winning the lottery ~
To help a friend in need.
To make someone smile and be happy,
With just a kind word or deed!

It doesn't cost a penny ~
To be civil and polite.
We should count our blessings daily,
And thank God every night!

Lynne Doyle

An Image Of Love

I look in the mirror and what do I see?
The person I love looking back at me.
I look in the mirror and what do I find?
A sweet smiling face that's gentle and kind.
I look in the mirror and to my surprise,
There's love shining out from those sparkling eyes.
I look once again, it's not a mirror at all.
It's my mother's photo that hangs on the wall.

Neata Todd

Modern Mouse

Remember the one about Christmas
And silence through the house
Where no creature was stirring
Including a mouse

Well since those words were written
Some things aren't the same
And most people have one
It's part of the game

In bedroom or study
Well all through the home
It's almost compulsive
Like your mobile 'phone

It helps you to access
To retrieve and store
Fancy a pie chart?
It helps you to draw

So let's pull a cracker
Put on your hat
It's ready for action
There on its mat

And with grandma and grandpa
And all through the house
It's just as important
The computer mouse

Val Stephenson

Rejected Love

You once held the key to my heart
We were both one, but now we're apart.
I loved you more than any other
But my feelings for you I had to smother.

Our love for each other was deep
But other seeds I dared to reap.
You belonged to another person
I fought with myself, I had to see reason.

I forfeited your love so true
For a false love that turned so blue.
I did for you what I thought was right
Life backfired, I lost the fight.

I think of you often with love
I looked for guidance from above.
There'll never be any love like yours
I rejected the key that opened my doors.

Linda Wright

All Terrain Vehicle . . . From Hell!

I went on my first ATV today,
Much to my stomach's dismay.
I can still hear the screeching brake,
Rather you than me, mate.
I became known as the 'English Bush Whack'
Because of my many journeys off track!
The sun is setting on the day,
And I'm storming along at about 20K,
Then all of a sudden, I hit a lump,
And into a tree, I land with a bump.
Out of the bushes, I climb,
I'm really OK, honest, I'm fine!
Once again our engines cruise,
I rub my leg and my *big* purple bruise.
So we carry on upwards, nearing the top,
But my eyes keep drifting to that immense great drop.
Finally we stop for a rest,
And upon my arm, I swat a few pests.
Then off we set once more,
Our tyres pounding on the dusty dirt floor.
We trundle on down through river and stream,
The sky occupied by single sunbeam.
'Take off ya brakes!' my sister yells in a huff,
'No thanks, I'm already going fast enough!'
I tumble over a few more rocks,
And give myself a few more knocks,
Then at last I see the base,
And a grin spreads across my face.

I kill my engine as soon as I can,
And jump inside the transport van.
'Anyone up for another ride sometime?'
The driver says as he turns the key,
And I reply, 'Well, we'll see . . .!'

Lyndsey Power

Out Of Reach

I miss you so much
I've missed you too long
Your face is everywhere
Your voice in every song.

The passion that was
The passion that could be
If only, my love, you were here with me.

Thoughts so deep and true
That I think about you
Cannot be expressed
They are kept hidden from the rest.

To carry on without you is so hard indeed
Just once more to see you is my greatest need.

My touch would be the softest of all
My voice would beg you to recall
The times we spent so tenderly
The closeness that was between you and me.

Others have tried but could not get close
It's you I've always loved the most
The love and hurt will not go away
So in my self-imposed exile I am destined to stay.

Lorna Marlow

Smokescreen

Lord, I've prayed to You in silence,
I've prayed to you out loud,
I've sent my prayers right up to You,
Wrapped up in a cloud.

Not a cloud that is Heaven sent,
But one of smoke and ash,
I've asked of You to help me out
'Cos these fags I smoke are trash!

I know Old Nick has hold of me
But I cannot break his grasp,
Lord, I'll keep on asking for Your help,
Right down to my last gasp!

You never seem to answer, Lord,
Perhaps You're waiting for me
To make some effort, of my own accord
Before I get help from Thee.

If I could give up smoking, Lord,
Yes, I'd be the one to brag
But the very thought so scares me stiff
I've just lit another fag!

Roger James Brawn

Sweet Love

Love is the sweetest thing
Always blossoms in the spring
Comes Cupid with his arrows
Sling into your heart strings
With a zing
Soon wedding bells
Begin to ring

K Morrison

Dad's Love In The Rainbow

Allow myself to open
Like a flower in the rain
Not wishing on a rainbow
To wash away my pain
Show the world some colour
Grow stronger every way
Show some rainbow colour

Show it! Today!

The windows of my heart
They are broken true
But there is a rainbow
Shining bright within me
Rainbow memories of you
To Heaven you went before me
Some time I have to spare
Until you come to greet me
Rainbow colour I must share.

Alison McColgan

Smiles

How many smiles does it take
To brighten up a room?
See the cheerful, happy faces,
Relieving all the gloom.

Smiles, like colds, can be infectious,
When caught are soon passed on,
Now everyone is smiling,
All the tension is gone.

The dark corners soon are lighter,
They almost seem to glow.
Such a change a simple smile makes,
Try it, then you will know.

They do say a smile costs nothing,
But worth its weight in gold.
So smile today at those you meet,
Friends, strangers, young and old.

Angela Pritchard

You

Your laughter builds the stars
Your smile makes them glow
You can make the sun shine bright
and the first spring flowers grow
You can stop the rain clouds
and make the rainbows shine
You can make the bluebirds sing
just by passing by

Your voice melts ice in the coldest hearts
Your face provides the sun
You can make the shadows hide
and the first spring deer run
You can take the hurt away
and make the lonely sing

With the strength of love in you
you can do anything

Emmalene Maguire

The Swan

Moving swiftly,
across the lake.
Ignoring the ducks,
and the fuss they make.
Gracefully floating,
not like the rest.
Who squibble and squabble,
the swan stays the best.

With beautiful feathers,
as white as snow.
The swan is their queen,
and don't they all know.
Forever and ever,
the queen she will be.
For she is the prettiest,
as you can see.

Katie Smith (13)

Time For Children

Seven children playing happily,
floor covered with their toys.
Singing, laughing and giggling,
sometimes making too much noise.
Piles of washing and knitting,
many favourite meals to cook.
Smart fashions are too costly,
mirrors do not need a look.

For illnesses, nursing mother,
whose skirt needs playful tugs.
Happily giggling and laughing,
arms full of cuddles and hugs.
Bubbly baths before bedtime,
Becky's not starting to teethe,
Nights are peaceful blessings,
with time to relax and breathe.

But then children are not photos,
to hang and admire upon the wall.
Children do have childish needs,
with God's love, we provide them all.
Well children are only children,
whether thin, ugly, cuddly or small.
Whether beautiful or handicapped,
with God's love, we love them all.

Joyce Dawn Willis

God's Anguish
(Based on Hosea 11:1-11)

To you birth I gave; to you a promise I made;
When you fell, I picked you up, held you on my knee;
When you were ill, I cared for you, with you I stayed:
I am here, reaching out to you, stay, stay with me.

Now you have abandoned me, turned to evil ways;
You have ravaged and slaughtered, earned the gallows-tree;
People rage against you, damn you all your days:
I am here, my arms are opened, turn, turn to me.

How can I give you up? How can I hand over you?
My love wells up; louder, louder grows my plea:
My anger will not last; what are we to do?
I am here, let us embrace and hope, hope with me.

Anger, torment, anguish, all these; yet love so near,
I am waiting, ready and opened, *I am here.*

    John A Mills

When I Was Joseph . . .

We must be made for each other, you and I,
'Cos I always laugh when you cry.
It'll be written on my epitaph, 'Me and Kerry'
'Cos when I was Joseph you were Mary.

Though we are too young to marry now,
We feel we must make a lovers' vow,
So as to assure that some day
Neither of us will go our separate way.
So we'll take a lock of each other's hair
And braid them with the vein of a bay leaf with so much care,
Seal it in a bottle; drop it in the Tyne,
So that forever you will be mine.
Our lives forever will float up and down
As the tide turns and spins around,
But together we will always be,
Twined together, like our token, with eternity.

We must be made for each other, me and you.
For the rest of my life I'll be saying, 'I do.'
See, I knew it was fate from our class Nativity,
When I was Joseph and you were Mary.

Rachael Mary Widdrington

Adoration

We move alone, the rooms are vast,
My thoughts are silent, impressed to last,
And with my feelings, I'll sign thy name,
Where feelings haunt, upon feelings flame.
Rapt soft winds moan through echoing towers,
Through shady vaults, through gilded towers,
Upon there our souls shall pledge to trust,
Uplifted upon the paths of dust;
Yet love and ray, shall sweep
Beyond all life's decay,
And hidden springs and words of power,
Will haunt through times transcendent hours,
But thee with such sentiment and eloquence,
To tower, will outshine upon times immortal bower.

Christine Hare

Stand In Lover

Green paths we walked
Hand in hand
For hours we talked
Our love so great
I had an ache

To not see her
Blinded my eye
To the day's toils
My work in a dither
Mind a quiver

I met her at eight
On my knee
I asked her my fate
'Will yu marry me?'

'No,' said she
'You're too late
I'm marrying thee mate
When he's back ~ from the sea.'

Roy Barker

Ode To Be Loved Again

Today I met this gorgeous boy
He seems so nice, I can't deny
Now I've known him quite a while
He puts me in a mood to smile
The years have passed and I still think
This gorgeous boy is mine for keeps
Although the years have rolled on ~ on
Love ~ it seems, has gone quite wrong
My love for him, has gone very wrong
He's turned from being a nice young man
To ~ a ~ very ~ jealous ~ one
He tells me that he loves me lots
But then the arguments erupt
My love has now turned to fear
As every day I'd like to disappear
And find that new love that once was here
He's out there somewhere, I know that
Because I've met this handsome man
I knew him many moons ago
When country music came to town
My love for music-man is very strong
We have a lot in common
Although he had to leave me in despair
Life's a bitch ~ I do declare
Perhaps one day, before I die
He'll wander back to me
And then who knows what will be
True love will have caught up with me
The torch I've carried all these years
Will turn to love again ~ you'll see

Myra Granville

John-Paul

He's strong yet gentle and stands so tall
My reason for living, my life, my all
He colours my day when I'm feeling sad
This is the son I never had.

My son 'John-Paul' would be like no other
We'd share a bond with one another
He wouldn't be perfect, no one ever is
Yet he'd know that the depth of my love was his.

We'd laugh a lot, my son and I
I'd share his dreams, he'd reach for the sky
As his life unfolds I would show him the way
To grow into manhood day by day.

The time would come when he'd take his place
A leader of men the world to face
I would bid him farewell and hide a tear
Though deep in my heart he'd be ever near.

My autumn years are drawing nigh
It will never be 'My son and I'
I could have carried the world with all its strife
Had I a son to enrich my life.

Bess Langley

So Many Ways

I love you in so many ways,
with every breath I breathe,
through all my days.

Each morning, when I see your face,
immediately, my heart
begins to race.

Your tender kiss, my lips cajole,
drawing me closer to you,
touching my soul.

You fill my life, so perfectly,
you are my rock, my strength
in adversity.

Quelling my melancholy tears,
and wisely, gently, sweeping
away, my fears.

No precious gold, or jewel bright
can outshine, the flame, that in
my heart, you light.

A lifetime! It would take you see,
to tell, of the many ways
that I, love thee!

Patricia Whittle

Flexible Love

It's amazing what love can take
Even without getting a break
Tempers hot, tears fall,
Words that hurt and that's not all.
Crashing doors, packing case
All because of losing face.
Male ego in full force goes
Venting forth of all its woes.
Female scorn at its best
Will never let a word rest.
All this can happen in one day
Except when love gets in the way.

Hazel Mills

Together

Nestle me softly
On a pillow of down.
Wipe up my tears
And smooth out my frown.
Hold my hand gently,
Enfold me caressing,
With words like soft music
And give me your blessing.
Tell me you love me
And always be there ~
To comfort, to hold and ever to share
The joy and the sorrow
That everyday brings
And together we'll conquer
The difficult things.

Judith Rawlings

Faith Can!

There's a problem in my life
And I don't know what to do,
I feel trapped between here and there
Not knowing what to choose.
I've tried so many times before
But I only seem to lose,
Although I've put my best efforts in
Or Lord! What should I do?

I know I have to change my will
And divinely follow You,
For it's in Your words of life
And I believe it to be true.
So why can't I turn from my own ways
And retire from this race,
Of limiting your promises
Instead of motivating my Faith.

Faith is the substance of all things
That I hope for in this life,
But for the evidence I must
Be prepared to sacrifice,
Imaginations, cast them down
And knowledge theories too,
To receive Your Holy Spirit
And be born again anew.

Now I know You hear me Lord
As I pray to You this day,
And I know You see my heart
And my struggles and dismay,
And You know it's hard for me
To believe what I just can't see,
But in You I will stand
And believe that my faith can.

Elaine Smicle-Thompson

Shadows In The Trees

Shadows in the trees as the sun filters through
As I walk in the bluebell woods with you,
The scented air, a patch of blue sky
Listening to birdsong in branches high.
Springtime in Devon, we find hidden flowers,
Jump earthy puddles from April showers.
Young man's fancy, old man's darling
Whichever it is in spring it is charming.
Chores done with pep, a quickening step
Spruced up to flirt with the one just met.
Who knows what the outcome will be
As I get to know you, and you get to know me?
In spring many others are doing the same
We smile and nod as we pass in the lane.
A shy kiss on the cheek to a friend that is new
In the shadow of trees as the sun filters through.

Patti Ryall

Rhyme Time

I think that it would be a crime
If what I write should fail to rhyme
For then, no matter how sublime,
The feeling would be lost in time.

And it would surely be unfair
If I released into the air
A rhythm that was hard to bear
For that would spoil my wish to share

My thoughts on subjects so diverse
As transport or the universe
For flowing harmony can reverse
The needless fears that make life worse.

Betty Nevell

Dreaming

I dream that he will smile at me and gaze into my eyes.
Just to hear him speak my name I'd be in paradise.
At a dance he'd hold me close, his arm around my waist.
I could stay there forever, held tight in his embrace.

I dream of walking with him through a woodland glade.
We'd lie on a carpet of bluebells, relaxing in the shade.
Or on a deserted beach, waves lapping on the shore.
We'd sit and watch the sunset: who could ask for more.

I dream of riding with him on the pillion of his bike.
Roaring through the country lanes, anywhere we like.
We could travel round the world, our spirits free as air.
As long as he was with me I wouldn't have a care.

I dream of being with each one, all of the day through.
But they're just stars on my TV screen, those dreams can't come true.
Maybe, one day I'll find the man who is right for me.
Until then, I have my dreams to keep me company.

Pamela Evans

A Rhyme In Time

How does the endless measure tread?
It doesn't matter how fleet our feet.
Can we ever hope to beat
The minutes hovering overhead.

Why did we ever invent the trick
Of making a treadmill for our race?
Relentlessly now the hours tick.
Forever we watch the clock's round face.

No plea can halt the beat of time.
Perhaps one day a discordant chime
Can conjure back a day sublime
When we dwelt in a happier clime,
Had time to find a more adequate rhyme!

Time is false, in a circular world.
Whirling upon it our bodies are hurled
At fabulous speeds we can't comprehend.
Thank God who has said it will one day end.

No more the scurrying ant-like battles
Shrilling alarm bells and constant rattles
Of millions of cog wheels, ratchets and pawls
Clocks on mantels, tables and walls.
I praise the eternal where time is dead
And I may sleep in my timeless bed!

Kath Aust

A Rhyme On Time!

It's 7.30am on a dreary morn
Wish I could stay tucked up in bed
However it's Monday, back to work
So I can pay for my daily bread

9.30am sit down at my desk
Letters to open, bills to pay
Cheques to bank, problems to solve
All make up a stressful day

11am no time for a break
Plumber not where he should be
Heating engineer wants more copper tube
Who can sort things, leave it to me

It's 1.30pm no time for lunch
Materials not arrived on site
Must hassle suppliers yet again
By 2.30 everything is put right

Time to concentrate on the quotes
As it's quiet between 2.30 and 3.00
Time to sort out the accounts
Then the power goes off in the factory

The contract costings require checking
The computer records need update
The phone never stops ringing
The VAT returns can wait

The faxes demand attention
It's 6.30 and I'm still here
Up to my eyes in paperwork
No time to have a cold beer

Carole Hackett

A Strange Recital
(This poem was written for and dedicated to Nurse Beverly Day, a Cumbrian lass, from Carlisle)

I've recited my poems to many strange faces,
I've recited them, too, in many strange places,
But a hospital trolley? Lying flat on my back?
No wonder the nurse seemed taken aback,
When I asked her a question, voice shaking with fear,
'May I recite you a poem, nurse? Will you listen my dear?'
And Nurse Beverly Day, for that was her name,
Responded at once with, 'Go ahead, Ralph, I'm game!'

So I recited my poem, about a rogue gene,
And the trouble it's caused me since I came on life's scene,
Then we both heard the click of an opening door,
And soft footsteps approaching across the floor,
Then the anaesthetist's voice spoke in tones firm but clear,
'Hello, Ralph, operation time is near!'
And a chloroform pad was then placed on my face,
Thus ending my recital in another strange place.

When next I awoke, I was back in my bed,
With an oxygen mask slipped over my head,
And with the effects of the chloroform now fading away,
From the foot of the bed I heard a voice say,
'You must try to relax, Ralph, no more poetry today,
Go for a long sleep, you'll feel better that way.'
And though I know I was in hospital for just a short stay,
I'm pleased that I met with Nurse Beverly Day.

Ralph C Davis

A Mixed Bag

The postman tramps along the road,
Carrying his bag ~ a heavy load,
He must work come rain or sun,
Beginning deliveries at number one.

The post is important, what will there be,
A dental reminder or a postcard for me?
A questionnaire, an electricity bill,
Special offers, are they sending them still?

He continues his round, there's no time to stop,
So many things in letter boxes to drop.
Charity appeals or forms to unravel,
Hospital appointments, brochures on travel.

A renewal notice, catalogue for a sale,
All sorts of items are sent through the mail.
New cheque books, statements from banks,
Party invitations, replied to with thanks.

But best of all, what we wait for or send,
Is a cheerful long letter addressed to a friend.

Joyce Buksh

Mugs Are For Coffee

Together a future
No really that's a laugh
The only place you led me
Was up the garden path

No bridal gown of satin
No platinum wedding rings
No frilly little bridesmaids
No other wedding things

No hen-night or honeymoon
Just a broken heart
I really should have listened
To my friends right from the start

They said you were an egotist
And that your heart was just for you
I'm just glad I found the truth
Before I said, 'I do.'

Gillian M Morphy

Time

If time stood still, there'd be more time
To do the things I like,
On sunny days I'd down my tools,
Across the fields I'd hike.
Or sit and ponder all day long,
About everything around,
Or play my music all the time,
Enjoying every sound.
I'd like to travel round the world
At a very leisurely pace,
And be quite unaware of this time scheduled life
That belongs to the human race.
I'd like to go back into time,
To see it all first hand,
The things I've read in history books
About this pleasant land.
But forward into time ~ No way,
To watch my life unfold,
And see it happening day by day,
This Woman growing old.

Margaret Whitton

Sport

Sport As A Lad

As a young lad I remember what sport was like,
excited I peddled fast on my rickety bike.
Be it football, cricket, or tennis that day,
I wanted to be early for the beginning of play.
My heroes I loved, and willed them to win,
their fair play and talent made me feel they were kin.
If they lost I admired their courage to accept,
they shook hands with the victor with genuine respect.
After the game there was great debate,
but no anger erupted at the outcome of fate.
The few that were nasty were quickly ignored,
bad sportsmen we hated no matter who scored.
We went home contented, the day had been fun,
it didn't really matter who'd lost and who won.

Sport As An Old Man

Sport as a lad? Alas long gone,
it's a business now, an enormous con.
I cannot afford to pay the fee,
sport is no longer for the likes of me.
Behaviour of players and fans alike,
is violent, brutal, with vicious spite.
Discussion gives way to aggressive fights,
fair play has gone, no one has rights.
The talent's still there, but seems tainted somehow,
if I admire a player it can cause a row.
I've lost interest in sport, in the modern way,
and relive the fun of an olden day.
I'm lucky, the memories are vivid and great,
the young can't compare, they were born too late.

Margaret McDonald

Their Gift

The silence is deafening
There is stillness all around.
A light breeze whispers
As I stand by the mound.

A man I did not know
But to whom we owe our freedom.
Who gave his life as a sacrifice
And we all never knew him.

The guns are now silent
The tanks no longer roar.
The bombs no longer fall
And the all-clear does not call.

There are no bombed buildings
No blackout curtains hung.
No rations needed now
No White Dover songs sung.

Brave men marched proudly
Willing to do their best.
Our country to fight for
But thousands were laid to rest.

Fresh eager faces marching
Tearful women looked on.
Some were wives and sweethearts
Most moms sent a son.

Children waved to daddies
Grandparents to a grandson.
Moms kissed their daughters
As nurses they now had become.

Terrible injuries they had to nurse
Heartrending screams were all they heard.
There were the ones who would just cry
And the ones they could not help would die.

Some shook violently
Too unsteady to stand
The nurses and doctors hoping
To help with skilled hand.

Some cried for sweethearts
Some for their mom.
Some slipped away quietly
Before anyone knew they had gone.

Here lies a quiet field
Blood-red poppies grow around.
A symbol to our brave people
Now nature is the only sound.

We must never forget
The misery war brings.
And the precious gift they gave us
Peace to enjoy all things.

    Sue Cockayne

Let's Dance

Let's dance.
Hold each other through the night so long
Turning to the tune of some sweet song.
Feel the music pulsing out so strong.
Let's dance. Let's dance.

Twisting round and round upon the floor.
You and me together evermore.
Let the music rain and let it pour.
Let's dance. Let's dance.

Moving to the rhythm and the rhyme.
Both of us together and in time.
Turning, twirling bubbles in the wine.
Let's dance. Let's dance.

We'll go dancing on and on and on
Sweetly stepping to the music's song.
Dancing till the last soft sound has gone.
Let's dance! Let's dance!

Pam Redmond

Blackbird

On topmost branch of naked tree
He perched, his head held high.
The breath of spring that fanned the air
As yet was weak and shy.
But as he stood upon his bough,
Eyes glistening with life,
Clear music from his beak arose
As sharp as whetted knife.
Towards the sun his note climbed steep ~
A shaft of utter joy ~
Soaring to conquest time and space
Vanguard of spring's envoy.
His lancet tongue vibrated with
The passion of his song.
His body moved in unison
His whole demeanour strong.
That special fleeting moment when
He opened wide his bill
Produced sound so exquisite that
Time faltered ~ and stood still!

Joan Tompkins

The Loner

I love to wander in a wood
For a loner I would be
In a place of solitude
Away from society.

With only squirrels and rabbits
And birds and flowers and trees
And bees and other insects
And grasses waving in the breeze.

I would sing a song out there,
With no-one near to hear
My woodland friends would listen
And frogs might linger near!

Woodland creatures are wonderful
Tho' their lives are fraught with danger
They are very wary
But to them I am no stranger.

Ages of persecution
By man with dog and gun
Have kept them very fearful
And ever on the run.

So please I say be kinder
And put those guns away
And let every woodland creature
Have its little day.

    Nan Downs

Clouds

Storm clouds surround the sky so black,
Why should we suffer all the flack?
It is predicted that we should
Do everything a body could.

To stay calm and reflect our minds,
On preventing any harm due to winds,
Race around pinning every moving thing
Securely to the ground, stop worrying!

Is there a patch of blue in the grey sky?
Surely there is a glimmer in the eye,
After the thunder and lightning has passed,
The clouds are dispersing en masse.

What a beautiful sight to see,
The clouds are racing ahead like a song,
Changing form as they flee,
In glorious flight sail along.

The storm seems a long way from here,
The panic has gone, now there is no fear,
The coast is clear, the water subsided,
No need then for us to be divided.

What a relief, we will not suffer grief,
Not this time, the storm was so brief,
There is a moral in this tale,
Be prepared for a further gale.

Mary Lawson

In Favour Of Rhyme

When I was a child at Mother's knee
Nursery verses she taught to me,
After repeating time after time
Easy remembered being in rhyme.

Recitations to be said aloud,
Family audience feeling proud
That a curly head of three years old
Such variety of verse could hold.

This pleasant pursuit has stayed with me,
It's quite obvious as you can see,
'Though into maturity arrived
Childhood's love of rhyming has survived.

They're not for me, other style of lines,
Free Blank Verse without any confines,
In striving to structure scan and stress
My efforts bring me such happiness!

Olive Miller

Impressions: Monday Morning; 9.35

Ashes lie on the table.
Dust lies on the floor.
Students talk in corners;
Of politics, life and lore.

Posters upon the wall,
Denoting seminars of various type;
Free drinks for the first hour on Friday:
And all the usual hype.

Tea in my cup lies cold.
My cigarette withered away.
Paper beneath my hand.
Thoughts on another day.

How I long to be this morning,
Sitting in the grass:
Watching daisies bend in the breeze.
Not part of this irksome mass.

Sandra MacLean

Wilfred

Sleek
Slender
Lost in the shadows
Apart from his eyes

Alert
Amber
Stealthily pounces
Elements of surprise

Playful
Purring
By my side
From the start

Wonderful
Wilfred
How quickly you
Captured my heart

Geraldine Laker

The Boy Whose Eyes Fell Out

I knew a boy
Who tried to see
The wind between the trees.

He stared so hard to see the air
That wasn't there
His eyes fell out.

And now he can't see owt.

    Mark Follows

Acceptance (Being Me)

'Not good enough,' I seem to hear,
'Not good enough,' I shed a tear;
Perhaps because I try to be
Someone who really is not me,
But Jesus loves me as I am.
He is my Shepherd, I His lamb.

If as myself I come to Him,
And not as Mary, Joan or Kim,
Just as I am, though often wrong,
I know to Jesus I belong,
And He will take me as I am,
For He's my Shepherd, I His lamb.

Now in my heart I have a song,
That I to Jesus Christ belong,
For He's accepted me, yes, me,
Just as I am so willingly,
However weak, however strong,
I know to Jesus I belong.

Anne Gray

Stop A While

Stop a while, and smell the roses,
The days, they pass so fast.
Stop, and smell the roses,
The perfume doesn't last.

Make the most of your children.
They are only on loan to you.
Their childhood years go quickly,
I know this to be true.

When I look back along the years,
Where did they really go?
My *little* son and daughter,
But all too soon they grow.

They've grown into lovely people,
I'm very happy to say.
I'm very proud, of both of them,
They're good citizens, today.

So, stop, and smell the roses,
As you pass along life's way.
If you stop, and smell the roses,
It will brighten up your day.

Jean D Smith

If I Only Knew

I look up at the sky at night,
There I see the stars shining bright,
Twinkling deep in oceans of space,
Mystifying the human race.
How did it happen years ago?
That's the secret I'd like to know.
Who created this majestic Earth?
Who gave us universal birth?

Telescopes peer deep into space,
Seeking signs of a living race.
Surfaces show signs of water,
This, we know, is life's supporter.
The Earth appears to be unique,
Other stars are barren and bleak,
Inhospitable, void of air,
Was there ever life present there?

Perhaps they came and went away,
Met our ancestors, who can say?
An advanced civilisation
Seeking out our forming nation.
Maybe their world advanced too far,
Perhaps I am looking at their star!
Some questions will remain unsolved,
Never, ever, to be resolved.

Ken Watts

Ode To Those Who Were Lost

There once was a land in turmoil,
Where evil stirred and brewed,
Where plans were hatched and plotted
And where people went without food.

But then came the saviours,
Brave and bright and tall,
They were prepared to face what lay ahead,
Hoping that good would not fall.

They fought against the darkness.
They fought along with the light.
They fought for the freedom of mankind.
They fought for all that was right.

The battle went on for what seemed like forever
And eventually Evil lost.
Good had triumphed overall,
But at a tremendous cost.

Lives were lost by the many,
Many loved ones had died in the frost
And so I recite this poem,
That is owed to those who were lost.

Gemma King

Dorothy Ann

With every tick of time
Of every dreary day
Heartache hills I climb,
Memories of you replay

Memories of youthful you
Light of my love affair
Wearing my favourite blue
Pure as the daybreak air

The church where we wed
Our fervent vows we gave
Till death do us part we said
There now I tend your grave

In the mirror of my mind
I hold your lovely face
Beauteous, sweet and kind
Angel of perfect grace

In deep despair
I reach for you in vain
No more a time to share
No more to touch again

In memory's treasured hoard
My life with you I scan
Golden days with my adored
Dearest Dorothy Ann.

Albert Cole

Good Times

Time is such a precious thing,
If you use it wise and well,
It makes the days and weeks go by,
It gives you a tale to tell.

Providing us with memories,
A passion we all should treasure,
Satisfying dreams gone by,
A unit beyond all measure.

Time can also heal a mind,
Or hearts when in despair,
It's strange that it can cure an ail,
Even though it isn't there.

Although it can make you happy,
There are times when it can make you blue,
Especially when so little of it,
Is spent sharing Time with you.

As years go by, memories age,
Time seems to go rotten,
Happy smiles and walks for miles,
I have not forgotten.

Although the little hand goes on,
And days seem to just fly,
We're still the very best of friends,
Aren't we, you and I?

Jo Williams

Why Is My Bag So Heavy?

Why is my bag so heavy? It sits on my shoulders like lead,
Filled with the flotsam of each passing day, it leaves me
                                        emotionally dead.
At seven o'clock, it was lighter, I picked up my bag from the floor,
Before that the whole world seemed brighter, now my burden is more
                                        than before.
At eleven o'clock it was heavy, I stumbled with every stride,
The bag is unbearably heavy by now, filled with something that I
                                        cannot hide.

Twelve strikes, but somehow I manage, to carry my load further on,
First I just ignore all my baggage, but soon all denial is gone.
I must try just a little bit harder, before all the pain overcomes,
So I grit hard my teeth, and I tremble, as the adrenaline each pain
                                        it numbs.
One-thirty, I rest for a moment, and try to forget all my pains,
As the strength of my soul suffers torment, and adrenaline courses
                                        my veins.

I open my bag and inspect it, discover just what lay inside,
The jumpers and socks must be made of rocks, the distance
                                        incredibly wide.
But my bag is devoid of all contents, the socks and the clothes that
                                        we share,
The feelings weigh more, more than ever before, but the heart of my
                                        bag it is bare.
I cover my eyes with my fingers, not knowing just quite what to do,
And the pain carries on, and it lingers, in my head is a picture of you.

It is three now, my journey's restarted, I can't see the end of my
quest,
Just trust in my bag, broken-hearted, and get to the end of my test.

The fruits of my journey is each passing hour, and when you're not
                                                    with me it's bleak,
For you are like nectar and bees to a flower, without which the plant
                                                    becomes weak.
It is four now, my bag is so heavy, I can't carry on any more,
My soul, my emotions, my being, lay scattered like stones on
                                                              the floor.

Rod Remnant-Ashton

I Met Him One Morning

I met him one morning
The day was just dawning
About three months old
He stood there in the cold

This went on for a while
From my door was about half a mile
He would wag his tail
As I posted my mail

I wonder how he found out
What time I'd be back
But each evening he was there
His back I would pat
He'd follow me home
Right to my door
And when I went in he'd offer his paw

At last I got bold
The weather was damp, wet and cold
I opened the door wide
He accepted the invitation and came inside

That was ten years ago
We loved each other I know
Through all those years
We roamed the moors
He really loved 'the great outdoors'

A few days ago
He was hit by a car
The driver didn't stop
By now is afar

The Vet shook his head
He's be better off dead
A few seconds thought
I had to agree
But oh! The look he gave me

So now I'm alone
Remembering ten years of love
From a pal I've known
Who is now up above

It started at a bus stop
Lasted ten years
I look back on much happiness
But cannot help a few tears

Les Parnell

Nemesis

Scenes of mayhem and disaster,
Foot and Mouth and BSE,
Man moving fast and even faster,
Travel carnage on TV.

Young folk out to test the waters,
Sexual licence, booze and drugs,
Parents see their sons and daughters,
Laugh it off with just a shrug.

Climate changes, droughts and flooding,
Ozone layer in danger too,
Ethnic cleansing, human cloning,
We've got ourselves in quite a stew.

Meddlesome man, no doubt believing
What was done was for the best,
Now we reap what we've been sowing,
Will we pass the final test?

God's creation finely balanced,
Teetering upon the brink,
Will we heed the global warning?
Or carry on until we sink . . .

Into the slime from whence
As science would have it
We came?

Vera Watson

Horn Of Plenty

Our journey down the winding Orinoco
Took us many months of sweating toil;
And as we rowed our cumbersome canoes
Through smoking film our skins began to boil
And itch. The river's noisome surface, skimmed
By flies and stagnant steam, stuck to our oars;
Mosquitoes danced before our smarting eyes,
While natives stood on Orinoco's shores

With grins upon their faces as we rowed.
The welcome here was primitive, but warm;
Our guide had gone before us to explain
Our pioneering zeal, although a swarm
Of mosquitoes prevented his return
By biting him all over. But the band
Of natives, ever friendly, took the lead
In showing us the place at which to land.

They ran along the shore towards a creek
Where, underneath a bower ~ a natural cage
Of overhanging boughs, a makeshift float
Of logs and branches formed a landing stage.
We came on shore, advanced a hundred yards
Into the trees, then gasped to see a horn
Of ivory suspended from a branch ~
A horn brimful of fruit. Its edge was shorn

Across the top; it dripped with honeydew
And richly overflowed with clementines,
Bananas, melons, plums and oranges,
Mangoes, mandarins and nectarines.
Such fare, provided by the colonists,
Was bliss. We ate our fill, then journeyed on.
But when the natives, having seen us off,
Returned with watering mouths, the horn was gone.

    Robert D Hayward

Cats
(Dedicated to our cats and Mark)

My cats are lazy; they sleep in the sun,
They do not want to play or have any fun.
Noodle is white, but not always clean,
Purdy looks after herself, she thinks she's a queen.
Bandit is dim, not right in the head,
When he gets scared, he runs under the bed.
Noodle is greedy he eats all the meat,
Bandit likes Munchies and Purdy likes sweets.
They all like cheese, which is good for me,
'Cause when I make my food; they help me eat my tea.

Suzanne L Shepherd

The Hard Part Of Art

In creating any kind of art,
following well-worn steps is smart,
to keep the horse before the cart.

An idea, a vision, must first dart
across your mind like a startled hart.
The general outlines next you chart.
Then you toil with all your heart
to shape and detail every part,
custom-tailoring, à la carte.
Beware embellishing like a tart.
Last, for grace, the polish impart.
All's to flow like oil, said Mozart.

Its adult life now ready to start,
let the work for the field depart
and, from its birthplace far apart,
joust with peers in the art-full mart,
taking on every counterpart:
serious, sweetheart or pop art,
by lionheart, artisan or upstart.

The hardest part of any art
is using its *blanche carte**
its competitors to outsmart,
leaving no worthy counterpart.

We trust our French reachers will not mind our reversing the order of these words English style. At least our carte *comes conventionally last.*

Roger Mather

The Ant-Agonist

'There's ants,' he said, that man of mine, 'In the Conservatory,
If they start having flights again they'll all be very sorry!'

Now, I like ants, to me they are a very civil specie,
Hardworking, very organised, their lives are far from easy.

I like to see the way they guard each precious egg that's laid
Whene'er a nest should be disturbed, such energy's displayed.

They rush about, it's just the same when 'Wedding Flight' is near,
Each winged 'intended' told to wait until *the day* is here.

Then off they fly and all is calm, I find it fascinating,
An aspect of the summer that is worth anticipating.

Though I'll agree if they appear inside the kitchen door
They get the order of the boot, 'Don't come in here no more!'

Now, as he does, my husband mowed the lawn the other day.
He lifted up the bird bath, *the whole street* could hear him say

'*An ant hill* underneath this bath, just come and have a look!'
The ants were running everywhere ~ who had the greater shock?

I had to pour a whisky for him ~ he the Stronger Sex,
You'd think he'd found a tiger, or Tyrannosaurus Rex.

I thought the ants should have a sip, but they were far too busy
For, true to form, they rallied round and moved house ~ made
                                                                    me dizzy

Watching this activity, but full of admiration,
I think reaction quite so fast should elevate their station.

I'll miss them in the winter, and I'll miss them in the rain,
But wait until next summer, then I'll greet them all again.

Then hubby will jump up and down, 'Those ants are back,' he'll say,
'Just have another whisky, Ken, and look the other way!'

    José Evelyn Wilcox

Taxi Driver

Cab for hire,
The clock is ticking,
Easy money,
Like pocket picking.

Flag him down,
In gets a stunner,
Drives her about,
She does a runner.

Takes the fares,
And make some money,
Drunken louts,
It's far from funny.

Dawn is breaking
Tank is empty,
Bag is bulging,
Sleep now . . . and plenty.

    P J Rowlands

Was And Is

Now that I've reached to age ninety-three
I'm looking back to how life used to be
People now seem in big hurry
The gobble up life and won't stop to worry
The roads were quiet where you walked each day
Now there is noise and you don't want to stay
The horses would pull the carts down your way
They didn't need petrol only oats and some hay
The coal fire was warm with a cheerful glow
The gas one was clean but no comfort would flow
Little shops have gone where we met like a friend
Now it's assistants who just want you to spend
Children learn quick their knowledge will last
Often you think they grow up too fast
Housework is easy with electric you use
And all is dependent on the model you choose
By telephone you speak to friends far away
And business is easy when you've no time to stay
Your arms, legs and liver could wear out that's true
Then clever doctors find new ones for you
You drink lots of medicine a cure you will make
And then one small tablet is all you must take
The tele brings the world to close where you are
Showing news and pictures from countries afar
People come here from other nations and creed
They all want a welcome and help in their need
Religion has changed with this modern view
We want to keep some of the old ways too
They say up there is safe with nothing to fear
But I hope I can stay a bit longer down here.

May Walker

My Love

My love is like the ocean,
he envelopes my soul.
Washing love all over me,
his gentle gestures let me see.
That I know without a doubt,
his love for me will not run out.
This man I love knows deep inside,
if I am ill or feeling tired.
Our souls are linked for him to be,
my shining knight who came to me.
He swept me off my feet one day,
and I'll never look back,
for he's here to stay.

Linda Sibley

Angel Eyes

Hidden from the world, this was fate
When my nephew arrived before the given date.
Small and precious with dangling feet
Love flowed, as much as, your tiny heart beats.

All you would do was sleep as you were helpless
Yet you came and brought such happiness.
Each time I held you, my love flowed deeply
An innocent angel who fell fast asleep.

You started to crawl across the floor
The ornaments have not been seen anymore.
It came a time when you wanted to walk
And sounds were heard as you even tried to talk.

You turned my life upside down
When you go home, there is an empty sound.
Your eyes glow whenever I am around,
With gurgling angelic sounds.

Abida Haidar

Bring Back Pictures In The Fire

Living-room fires used to dictate which way to face.
Now hordes of televisions have taken their place,
Shaping how we arrange the chairs
While distracting us from our cares.
On today's mantelpiece, above the screen,
As usual, plants and greeting cards are seen.
And the box resembles an old friend
Which, should we at times to slumber tend,
Like an indulgent pal, doesn't mind,
Sleep being not all it helps us find.
We saw pictures in the fire in days of old,
A plus freely added to relief of cold.
So are scenes contrived with skill and sent to lure
Less boring? Frankly, viewers aren't always sure.

Allan Bula

Eve Of Construction

Our future is predicted
A code has been revealed
will the sceptics be convicted
or truth again concealed?

Encoded prophets meaning
but God has since replied
a cruel computer screening
which cannot be denied.

A wordsearch may be faulted
but the writing's on the wall
a cynic's jeer is halted
before his rise and fall.

Earth's received its warning
all Nations are addressed
mere signs of madness scorning
which cannot be suppressed.

The key is real repentance
for in the final hour
God will then pass sentence
And He will show His power

To an evil generation
only Jonah is the sign
and miracle of healing
with water into wine.

A new eve on destruction
a new millennium brings
A challenge for construction
'ere the ending of all things.

Down through time and history
predictions have come true
this only leaves a mystery
the next one could be *you!*

Judy Studd

Rhyme In Time

Hours, minutes, seconds
Time flies by.
Days, nights, weeks, months ~
Away the years fly.

Tick tock goes the clock
The sundial marks the shadows.
My watch regimentally continues to lock
Yesterdays into tomorrows.

A rhythm in time
No time to rhyme
Amid all the hustle and bustle.
From time to time
Life seems to rhyme
But mostly the rhythm is rustle.

Den Evans

Progress

Tramping and rambling down the lane
Passing horses with flying manes,
In the background tall metal cranes
In the eye of the beholder, such pain,
Standing in the dreary rain
Thoughts running like a train,
To lose all this, there was no gain
Nothing would ever be the same.

Fields and hedgerows lose their claims
To these giant awesome frames,
Drillers and diggers it seems like a game
They keep the same beat, again and again,
They are killing the Earth deep down to its brain
The holes are so deep, in goes the drains,
It looks so forlorn now, just mud-covered plains
This small part of beauty has now been slain.

Mary Neill

The Scone Song

Last year whilst on vacation in a quaint old seaside town,
I came across an old tea-shop, went in and sat right down.
A waitress came to serve me, her apron starched and white;
She offered cakes and fancies, choux pastries and delights.

I gazed o'er this choice of treats which met my eyes with ease,
And settled for a home-made scone, *'I'll have one of those, please.'*
She brought it to my table, it had jam and butter on;
She placed it right in front of me and said, *'Enjoy your scon.'*

'What is that you said just then?' I thought I'd heard her wrong,
She said, *'I said 'scon' just then. Did I say something wrong?'*
*'No, my dear, there's nothing wrong, please don't mistake my tone,
It's just that you said 'scon', whilst I call this a 'scone'.'*

   Waddington Minge

A Rhyme In Time

As I get older, I seem to be
Gradually, discovering, me
The days of my youth, just starting out
I didn't know, what life was about
Then came marriage, and responsibility
Others to think of then, you see
Sadly widowed, start again
My equilibrium, to regain
Again, I married, but sadly, for me
Widowed, once more, I turned out to be
Once again, I had to restart
After a second, broken heart
Then, just after that, in time
I started, to write, in rhyme
What a blessing, sent to be
A real, 'God send', to me
Now, I think and write, in rhyme
Every day, and, all the time
A new horizon, just for me
To set my mind, and spirit, free
I read them out, on the radio
And others, in publications, go
I write for occasions, and for friends
I hope inspiration, never ends
At last, I've found in poetry
Something that is, wholly, me
A rhyme, in time, most certainly
A rhyme, in time, it turned out to be

Joyce Metcalfe

Times Gone By

Oft have I wondered
of times gone by,
a very warm summer
and a lovely blue sky,
walking with friends
in the cool evening shade,
listening to the cattle lowing
down in the glade,
wild geese flying
high in the sky,
when you're contented
doesn't time fly by.

Robert Gerald

Don't Know It, Poet

Wouldn't it be fun
If when we converse
We said everything
In poems and verse
Like, 'How are you?'
'Well, I'm alright.'
'Shall I meet you
In the pub tonight?'
'Of course I'll come
But don't tell the wife
Say it's a union meeting
Or she'll have my life.'
And there's, 'Mum! Mum!
Where's my favourite shirt?'
'On the floor where you left it
All covered in dirt.'
And, 'Did you do your homework?'
Said teacher, all stern
'Of course Miss,' says pupil,
'For I want to learn.'
I'm feeling quite dizzy
What's wrong with me?
I think I'll sit down
And make a nice cup of tea
Like measles it's catching
You can't stop the rhyme
It makes everyday language
Great fun all the time.

June Davies

Ode To Mr Forrest ~ A Lousy Driver

A car when it's cared for
And given the right food
Is often quite useful
When in the right mood
It has often been known though
To dent in the flank
When carelessly handled
Or used as a tank.

They say that a car
Shows the size of a man
I think then in that case
Mr Forrest's a van.
If accidents happen
And your car, is flawed
Just pray that it's his fault
And you're strongly insured.

Vivienne Rae Nolan

At The Airport

Stifling heat, bags and cases,
Long, long waits, last embraces,
Steps and lifts and escalators,
Trolleys, pushchairs, perambulators,
People, people whirling through
Watching arrows just like you.
Signs to follow ~ look around
Until the check-in desk is found
At the airport.

Passports, tickets, labels, pen ~
Now we're rid of luggage then
We're told departure time's
Been put on hold ~
Fifty minutes more to wait,
Head towards departure gate.
Lots of time for airport shopping ~
Suntan lotion, ties and shades,
Radios and razor blades
At the airport.

Drinking coffee, munching Mars,
Maybe using airport bars,
Browsing book racks, filling time.
'Ping!' ~ announcing flights to leave
One or two hours late, perceive!
Vacuous faces now resigned
To wait another extra hour
Watch ride-on hoovers glide the floor
On yet another cleaning tour
Steered by staff in zombie boredom
At the airport.

Phil Harvey

I Wish

I wish I could bottle
the wonderful smell
of a field of newly mown hay

Or the smell of a garden
after rain
on a really hot summer's day

I wish I could bottle the 'Autumn Smell'
when wood smoke fills the air
Or the smell of winter
frosty and cold
when foxes stay close to their lair

I would love to bottle
that wonderful smell
The smell of the salty sea
I would keep this with me always
It would be a favourite for me

Jenny Brownjohn

Rhyme

I walked with time
and found that
she is not measured
by our empty precision
but rather
she must be treasured

in every leaf and flower
that blooms and fades,
where reality and memory
are more than we
can measure, where
what is, is more sensory

than what we thought.
For time is not the boring
journey of hands across
a face, but rather
knowing where we've
been but at a loss

to know where we have
still to go. Ask each sun
rise why it sets.
Listen to our wild world
and know why we grow.
Learn time's alphabets.

John Clancy

In Such A Place

The village now is far below,
Its sounds have died away;
All round me spreads the open Vale
Upon this summer day.

The swaying heads of ripened corn
Sigh softly in the breeze;
The hills lie smooth against the sky,
Above the distant trees.

A skylark fills the air with song,
A glorious clear cascade;
Around the old half-hidden barn
The cattle search for shade.

The grass stands high along the lane
That winds towards the hill;
The hemlock dances in the breeze
And then once more is still.

In such a place, at such a time,
Eternity seems near;
The world is left behind, and yet
A truer world is here:

In such a place, at such a time,
Are broken things made whole;
God's presence is around me here,
And peace is in my soul.

Peter English

A Hebridean Holiday

We had sailed away from Oban
Past the isles of Skye and Mull
The crossing had been a little rough
And the sky and sea were dull.
But then I saw a band of light
Rising up, ahead of us.
Were we sailing into Heaven?
Could I hear an angels' chorus?
The angels were the seagulls
Come to welcome us to stay
And there, in sparkling sunlight,
Stood the town of Castlebay.
A wondrous sight I've yet to see
I can recall it every day
Through the memories in my photographs
Of my Hebridean holiday.

Sara Newby

Autumn Clean-Up

There is a fieldmouse
In my greenhouse
On the ground there is a slug
Slithering on the mud
Lifting up the pots and pails
Ugh, there are many snails.

All around are cobwebs
Upon the grass and flower beds
Daisies, buttercups, thistles, weeds
Growing fast, without planting seeds.

There is digging to be done
This work is not much fun
Putting fertiliser on the ground
Causing a fine stench all around.

Snowdrops, crocus, tulip bulbs
Ready to put in
Waiting for a fine display
Of flowers in the spring.

Hedges to be trimmed
Long grass to be strimmed
Following up with the electric mower
Then tidying the garden bower.

Paths and patios to be swept
So much to do I am out of my depth
Rubbish built into a pyre
Ready for a big bonfire.

Irene Pierce

Time

In times of yore ~ not so very long ago
Help in neighbourhood went to and fro,
And people found time to stop and chat
Of cabbages, kings ~ this and that.

These times we have leisure more and more
Yet mostly do not know the folk next door,
We are all so very busy ~ being busy,
We rush about in a constant tizzy.

Many machines save time these days
Convenience food saves time in other ways,
For all time saved whom should we thank?
We cannot save it ~ as in a bank!

What do we do with this time saved?
Does it make us better behaved?
Do we spend time helping each other?
~ Or is it simply too much bother?

Could we but return to an earlier time
As in the days of grandmother mine,
When folk worked hard the live long day
Yet still found time to help and play.

Gwen Mason

A Rocket For Guy

In 1605, on the fifth of November,
'Guy', was his name, folks will remember,
Loaded his powder, and headed for town,
Hoping to bring, the Government down,
Roll out the barrel, have barrels of fun,
Blowing the lot, to Kingdom come.

But alack and alas, and hey nonny no,
James the first, was aware of it all,
Whispers in lobbies, that sort of thing,
Leaks had reached, the ears of the King.

So he sent for the Sheriff, and had him arrested,
And after a trial, when all had attested,
Guilty was he, when the Jury retired,
Convicted of treason, for having conspired.

And ever since then, on the fifth of November,
We've never forgotten, we've always remembered,
And set him alight, on the top of a fire,
Not for the treason, or having conspired,
It's simply revenge, on him and his lot,
Who made such a botch, of the Gunpowder Plot.

Samantha Warburton

For Her

For her I'd pen the finest words
Like golden spun embroidery
Thread the weave from my soul
Commit myself emotionally.

For her I'd wish to scale the heights
Challenge the roar of wind and sea
Be the flower of chivalry's knights
To be more than I should be.

A jewel cut from the morning sun
I'd set delicately in her hair
A silken shift for her form
More delicate than evening air.

For her, for her, I'd bind my heart
And dream one single dream
Douse other flames, fancies forget
Forever dwell in springtime green.

Mike Monaghan

A Faraway Land

Once upon a time in a faraway land
A creature was found buried deep down in the sand
He was big and green with one red spot
Which if touched grew very hot
People came to stand and stare
How had it got here and from where
Maybe it had dropped from the sky
It was far too big to put in a pie
Perhaps it crawled out of the soil
No pans that big to put it in to boil
Where to put it they began to ponder
It wouldn't fit on the back of a Honda
The people got tired and they all went home
Leaving the creature all alone
When morning came the creature was gone
And all that was left was a terrible pong

Jackie Annetts

Tangled Love

He can't see my thoughts.
My dreams are my own.
His feelings are so disguised
that my heart feels alone.

I need his thoughts
am I in his dreams?
How do I know how he feels
if I don't know what his smile means?

A tangled love affair
between this guy and my mind.
Confusing messages.
No certainty of any kind.

Shall I keep my secret
or tell him my thoughts?
Do I realise my dreams
and risk getting caught?

Charged with lust
and love in the first degree
what happens if he doesn't
feel the same way about me?

Amanda Clapp

Berwick Church, Sussex

Tread gently on this hallowed ground,
pause a while, then look around,
between rolling Downs and green-leafed tree
tell me now, what do you see.

A small Church rising from the ground
upon a one-time leafy mound,
where a thousand years ago 'tis said,
the ancient people laid their dead.

Nearby lean half-buried crosses
and aged tombs with creeping mosses
and when the sun begins to fall
the shadows cool the crumbling wall.

The door is open, let's enter in
the Church is still, no choir boys sing,
through lattice pane the sunbeams stream,
and now behold the exotic scene.

Upon the walls in a brilliant hue
a life-like Christ looks down on you,
in colours rich the Angels fly,
a tribute to the artist's eye.

This little Church you've just been in
through the ages echoed Psalm and Hymn,
it sets the hearts of all aglow,
as did the works of Angelo.

R Cunningham

Grandad

Grandad, I loved, but has now gone forever,
My heart aches for him, but, I know I will never,
Forget to remember how good he was to me,
A friend who cared and loved me for me.

He cheered me up when I was down,
And had enough love to go all around,
He was one of a kind in every way,
And in my heart he will always stay.

And when the times comes for us to unite,
Our love will have grown to a greater height,
Nothing will come between our love,
Even through the good times and rough.

Grandad, I loved, but, has now gone forever,
My heart aches for him, but, I know I will never,
Forget to remember how good he was to me,
A friend who cared and loved me for me.

Karen Lawson

Tiger

Walls of concrete
Bars of steel
Does anyone know how you feel
Pacing round this way and that
Settle down rest on your mat.

Strong snarling jaws
Powerful paws
What lies behind your eyes of fire,
Beauty of form that I admire
If I had the right
I would take you where your mind races.

To your home of trees and lakes and hidden places,
Eyes that lead your way in the darkness you would grow
In strength and majesty
Where nature intended you to be

Not caged but free
The stripes on your coat and long swinging tail,
Gleam in the sun
As you watch the tormentors by the rail
People watch they pass you by
You watch in awe
Your heart is sore
As they watch, you watch them
They are thankful
For the bars of steel
But have they ever stopped to think how you feel.

    M Campbell

The Oboe Player
(Dedicated to my son, Robert, who although a fine musician, preferred a career in Geo-Chemistry)

I heard an oboist play today,
He played a sad refrain,
He's going to a new world,
And leaving home again.

He's travelling to Australia,
To make himself a name,
To play his oboe solos;
To play his way to fame.

He'll play with different orchestras,
In cities large and small,
He'll meet with fine musicians,
In every concert hall.

And when he plays a Mozart concerto,
The one that was composed in C,
The halls will be hushed and silent,
Scarce a dry eye will there be.

And as the music slowly dies away,
The audience will clap and cheer,
He'll take a bow on the platform's edge,
Wipe away a wayward tear.

Then he'll play in Western Australia,
At the Royal Concert Hall in Perth,
Before flying back to England,
To the country of his birth.

And when he reaches home again,
He'll be greeted with acclaim,
As an oboist of distinction,
Who has played his way to fame.

Ralph C Davis

A Lily's Gilt

A lily's leaf tinged with gold foil
Is not dross from a barren soil.
The golden leaf a symbol is
Of love's passion sealed with a kiss;
Not lovers in a sharp recoil.

An artist painting on the boil
His golden picture's rich through toil;
Wholesome in times of crisis 'tis,
A lily's gilt.

The wealthy man trapped in a coil
May set up others to embroil,
Corrupted by unhallowed bliss
Whose core is wanton and remiss:
A wicked life set to despoil
A lily's gilt.

Angus Richmond

The Weekend Break

As we drove through the pass to Llanberis
Saw the hills and the valleys so deep
I'll always remember the sight of
The mountains and all of those sheep.

As we finally got close to Snowdon
A beautiful sight to behold
The sun sparkled high on the mountains
And none of us noticed the cold.

The weekend was really quite magic
The food, and the sights all around
But nothing had really prepared us,
For that wonderful, wonderful sound.

The voices of a choir in the foyer
Male voices so deep and so strong
So wondrous, a joy, full of laughter
The Choir were all in full song.

We joined in some songs, then we listened.
Impromptu, a concert so fine,
We ladies from Notts were enchanted,
At the music, so clear and divine.

As for making our weekend so special,
We chatted and told little tales
But one thing that made it exciting
The music and voices of Wales.

Eileen Burton

The Now

It's with the tears of yesterday
To water the roses with which we say
Thank you for each and every day
That we have with the ones we love
To be in pain in our early years
To build strong bridges to cross rivers of tears
Has brought us safe to the other side
Where there's love and trust with no need to hide
You will now blossom in the sun
With friends, your children and everyone
Who sees you as you really are?
Beyond the thoughts of your own fears
They have helped you throughout the years
To be just as you are for all to see
A girl seeking a woman to be
You have been there for a time gone by
It was hard to feel what you or I
Could feel within your soul
To hold you once then let you go
For with the Eagles you must now fly
As there is one that is drawing nigh
To hold you in his hands
For you alone now can see
That the path you travel is free
Of old scars and fears thrown in your way
Clear, clear with no sins today
To be at one with love fulfilled
Yes you may go as a little child
In wonder and in awe
Enjoy your life forever more

    Yenti

Friends

Friends are the ones you can always rely on,
They'll always be there with a shoulder to cry on.
Willing to listen when you need to talk,
Will come for a drink or just for a walk.

Night or day they will always be there,
Someone to be with, or someone to care.
Friendly advice they are willing to give,
They'll always come up with 'a reason to live.'

There's no need to be lonely, just pick up the phone,
Or jump in the car and drive round to their home.
There's always a welcome, there's always a smile,
Even if busy, they'll stop for a while.

Even with problems of their own,
They'll never make you cope alone.
Their problems will quickly be pushed out the way,
They can be sorted out some other day.

Nothing on Earth will ever compare,
Only one thing will always be there.
True friendship is precious, so don't let it go,
Everyone needs it much more than they know.

Marisa Greenaway

Reflections On The Millennium

If we consider when the world began,
Two thousand years is little in the universal plan.
Man has evolved over thousands of years,
But now guns and bombs have replaced his spears.
He has more knowledge, more technical skills,
Yet the one thing he lacks is curing men's ills!
There's still many people without water or home.
Yet millions were spent on a Millennium Dome.
So many are hungry and live in great fear,
Whilst we in the West celebrate that great year.
What is the answer I ask you and me,
How long must it take to bring harmony
To a world that is rife with conflict and greed
Whilst some have much more than really they need?
So many Leaders are thirsty for power,
Beginning with promises that somehow go sour.
So, now that we celebrate this Special Birth,
Let's pull together and value our Earth.
Let's get together forgetting our hate,
Let's stand together, before it's too late!

Joan Leahy

Live For The Day

It is my wish to write a rhyme about the spectacular
Pembrokeshire Coast.
Of so many exhilarating coastal walks and pathways it can boast.
From the cliff tops one can gaze with rapture at long stretches
of golden sandy beaches.
And watch the power and the energy of a storm and hear
the seagulls' harsh, loud screeches.
The wonders of nature miraculously unfolds and charms
and beguiles the beholder.

A sunny day beckons me towards the lily ponds,
where I love to leisurely amble.
And on the bridge spanning the ponds I hesitate
and admire the Water Lily's picturesque ensemble.
Such delight as a gorgeous Woodpecker swoops, silently and swiftly
and without too much effort, snaps a darting dragonfly.
The faint-hearted cries out in alarm, but these priceless
and precious moments of nature flashed right in front of one's eyes.
As I turn the bend, the dazzling sea and soft gentle sands
of Broadhaven welcomes me with outstretched arms.

I have so many unforgettable memories of sun-drenched carefree
days of my children's light-hearted laughter like free spirits
riding the waves, building boats and moats and being hypnotised
by the sheer beauty and peace of Barafundel Bay.
This idyllic glimpse into paradise made it difficult to tear one's self
away, also Swan Lake was another secluded beach with a pretty bay.
The sand dunes at Freshwater West was an ideal playground for my
children to hide and play.
The Pembrokeshire Coast and the little village of Manorbier,
will forever remain special and dear.

Elizabeth Myra Crellin

The Tooth Fairy

When I was a little boy,
Little things would give me joy.
Whenever I would lose a tooth,
In the innocence of youth,
To gain a sixpence I would try,
But failure always made me cry.
Wartime sirens by night and day
Scared the tooth fairy right away.
My teeth are false, now I'm older.
I thought that I would be bolder.
I set my teeth beneath the pillow
To gain all my silver in one go.
As you've guessed, she didn't come near
And I got bitten on the ear.

Graham John

A Birthday Thought

Birthdays offer the opportunity to look back and to reflect
On the days and months and years that have gone by.
The successes and disasters, the happy and the sad
And the times that you can't really quantify.
It's all part of life's rich pattern; your personal tapestry
Of memories entwined to make a whole.
Of occasions you've planned carefully with love and tender care
Plus events over which you've no control.
But it isn't that important what has happened in the past,
It's the way that you respond to circumstance.
As you learn from past experience your character is formed
And in retrospect perceive the relevance.
As you reminisce upon your life you'll realise it is true
Success isn't measured in what you've done,
But by the people who love you.

Pauline Cunningham

Within Verona's Walls

Young lovers then but many years have passed
Since first we roamed around those pink grey walls,
Yet time flies as the Adige flows fast,
So close your eyes and dream before dusk falls.

In deepest dark of night well set the scene.
A love duet sung soft on centre stage,
In Piazza Bra the pas de deux unseen,
A couplet of endearment from the sage.

Let's reminisce and muse on days gone by,
Of Romeo and Juliet, of joie de vie.
Across the Old Stone Bridge we'll climb up high,
For on St Peter's Hill, I'll rest with thee:

> Within Verona's Walls to be as one,
> Kissed by the moon and warm Italian sun.

George Puttock

City Of Fear

As I walk through the busy City Streets,
Tanks buzz round, Like giant bees.
The grey dusk sounds a Curfew Bell,
Our Limbo, Between Heaven and Hell.
Jaws of Evil ~ Bite into the Heart,
Tearing Man ~ And Brother wide apart.
Deep in my City Dark, With fear,
My Countrymen draped in Riot Gear.
Wolves in Sheeps' clothing, Stalk our Streets,
A Nation Depressed, As History repeats.
As I look through the window ~ of the past,
Recall the suffering, On my Nation cast.
Through Concentration Camps ~ And wires barbed,
Where Millions of my People Died or Starved.
Oh to live in Glasnost and in peace,
Love ~ And raise my Family, With Joy and ease.
We know not Liberty, It's never been ours,
My Nation suppressed, In a Monster's Claws.
May God help us to find a Peaceful way,
To live our lives in Freedom, Day by Day.

Mary P Linney